PENGUIN MODERN POETS 16

JACK BEECHING was born in 1922, was brought up in Sussex, and served during the war. Since then he has spent much of his time abroad, chiefly in Spanish-speaking countries. He is a professional writer, but his main concern is poetry. For a while he was Poet in Residence at North Dakota State University. In 1969-70 he received a grant from the Arts Council of Great Britain. His books of poems are: *Aspects of Love, Truth is a Naked Lady,* and *The Polythene Maidenhead* (from which this Penguin selection is taken). *Poet as Conspirator* is a critical work. Jack Beeching is currently editing Hakluyt's *Voyages* for the Penguin English Library.

HARRY GUEST was born in Penarth, Glamorgan, in 1932. He was educated at Malvern and Trinity Hall, Cambridge, where he read Modern Languages. As a post-graduate at the Sorbonne he wrote a thesis on Mallarmé. From 1955 to 1966 he taught first at Felsted, then at Lancing. In 1966 he took up an appointment as lecturer in English Literature at Yokohama University. The long poem *Private View* appeared in 1962 and since then he has had three collections of poems published – *A Different Darkness* (1964), *Arrangements* (1968), and (poems written in Japan) *The Cutting-Room* (1970). His wife is American and they have two children.

MATTHEW MEAD was born in Buckinghamshire in 1924 and served in the army from 1942 to 1947. He edited the little magazine *Satis* and has published two books of poetry: *Identities and Other Poems* and *The Administration of Things.* He is now living in Germany and is married to Ruth Mead, with whom he has translated: *Shadow Land* by Johannes Bobrowski, *Generation* by Heinz Winfried Sabais, *Amfortiade* by Max Hölzer, works by Bienek, Borchers and Bächler, and some of the poems of Nelly Sachs.

Penguin Modern Poets

—— 16 ——

JACK BEECHING
HARRY GUEST
MATTHEW MEAD

Penguin Books

Penguin Books Ltd, Harmondsworth, Middlesex, England
Penguin Books Inc., 7110 Ambassador Road, Baltimore, Maryland 21207, U.S.A.
Penguin Books Australia Ltd, Ringwood, Victoria, Australia

—

This selection first published 1970

—

Copyright © Penguin Books Ltd, 1970

—

Made and printed in Great Britain by
C. Nicholls & Company Ltd
Set in Monotype Garamond

Contents

HARRY GUEST

MATTHEW MEAD

ACKNOWLEDGEMENTS

The poems by Jack Beeching are from an unpublished collection, *The Polythene Maidenhead*. Grateful acknowledgement is made to the author, c/o Hope Leresche & Steele, 11 Jubilee Place, Chelsea, London SW 3.

The poems by Harry Guest are taken from *Arrangements*, 1968, and *The Cutting-Room*, 1970, both published by Anvil Press Poetry.

The poems by Matthew Mead are selected from *Identities and Other Poems*, 1967, published by Rapp & Whiting; *The Administration of Things*, 1970, published by Anvil Press Poetry.

JACK BEECHING

FOR THOMAS McGRATH

Dodo is Dead

A quarry takes a bite out of a hill;
Shot whale turns belly uppermost; fake star
Intones an orbit; chimney sirens cry:
Labour is holy! Profit is better than prayer!
Fish in fetid rivers die;
Dodo is dead.

In a secret clinic, two-headed monsters weep;
In his penal battalion, the poet scrubs a floor.
Which of those numbered demijohns was Mother?
Which of those taboo faces might have been God?
Verses for tapers;
Dodo is dead.

Or innocence, considered as a market
In ruin. Or the contraband in love:
The last young lovers, handcuffed plunderers, kneel;
The men in harness lunge their lecherous clubs.
Hymen is a horselaugh; listen:
Dodo is dead.

In the penthouse strongroom of their maximum tower
A maniac is choked to death with money.
Down in the basement, dwarfs are burning sobs,
Dead fish, a membrane, monsters, broken flowers.
Curious ash blows upward:
Dodo is dead.

And Then Again, They May Not

And then again, they may not; then again
The reputations, and the walls, come down
In one fat pile; the sun dust fall so deep
Logic and ledgers go; from eye to eye
Her holy forehead smeared, the former mouth
Thick as a piecrust; breathing, of course, over.
Then again, they might not; then again.

Or if they did, or if they only would
Drown us in honey, smother it with cream;
Deep, deep the trees go laughing, and this laugh
Becomes the usual way to say goodbye.
Skyhooks and sacrifices prop the sky
(Puff clouds, and bathe in snow, and eat the sun)
Or, if they did, or, if they only would;

But then again, they may; and say they did
Chop toes and fingers, push out eyes like plums,
Such virgins as there may be, rape, such kissing
(Shutters like eyelids, eyes like windows gape)
Call treason, as the heavens and houses fall;
Or, if they did, or if they only would;
But then again, they may not; or they might:

Love, that is, only love. But then again
Eros and agape are difficult.
And then, they may; and say, and say, and say.

This Dark Night

Wiped blade on mane, struck hilts on doors;
The newborn had outlandish eyes,
Men months after loathed their wives.

Now enter town like dolls in trucks.
Guns at crossroads kill the street;
Lies envenom all who breathe.

Official menaces confirm
What literates feared: that technical
Is another term for dead.

What damns is never lust, but guilt:
Once yielded, with a cuckold shrug
The winter city cries for bread.

White faces move across the plain;
In the wilderness, dream of fire.
The knack of giving help is lost.

Some day ends the temporal waltz
In a whirl of anger, a clap of hands.
Leap, rider, into this dark night.

Love as a Siege

Defenders were desperate, had a pain in the neck
From the chronic act of looking. The besiegers
Came on as ever, behind a column of mirrors,
Old-fashioned myrmidons under their tufts of hair;

And when bombarded bastions lifted and fell,
If men craved men, inordinate women came
(Vaults blown skyhigh). Girls eager enough for dildoes
Were caught up in their own unbuckled flesh.

That line of mirrors made a joke of rape.
The perforating pain was like a dream
More luminous than love, more brilliant
Than hellish chocolate masking white ice-cream.

Conceived that day by oppositional wit,
Who poisoned cisterns? Let the cellars run
Waist-high in mother's blood? Those innocents,
Toppled like dominoes, puffed like opium;

Have monkey, chorister, fencible in them,
Wear filibegs, love fireworks, drift at night
Through black-eyed streets to the same old ruined wall,
Parley with strangers, part their knees for drunks;

And granny, too, will squat across the gun
In that ancient breach, to egg a foreigner on.
Has her fusty wig been sprouted by the moon?
Have you worn your best face lately, the kissing one?

Several Ways of Dying

Like taunt, and then caress,
Knife gives a personal thrust.
Two bare and furious hands
Choke, human as a kiss.
Gun is the harlot one
And counterpart of lust.
No living flesh withstands
Her stroke of artifice
Or outrage of excess.

Gun symbolizes all
That murder from afar:
Counterfeit embraces;
Bombs, or falling fire;
The fantasies of bliss
Or harlotry of power.
What stricken lovers are
Choking, kiss by kiss,
They'll strangle: their desire.
Yet feel no carcass fall.

Spread on a Wheel

Spread on a wheel for birds to perforate,
Hair weathervane, her ribs a punnet of wind,
Left hand is talon, but the lolling right
Drops knuckles, autumn nuts too desiccate
For teeth to crack, too bare for carrion crow.

What are you doing up in the air, my love?
Doll on a steering wheel, distressing shape
On the skyline of a Reformation master?
Why should my farded mascot drop her bones,
Become rats' castle, chassis, total disaster?

Why are you moping down there on the ground,
Surviving lover, tripes in a sack of skin?
Haven't you heard of living close to nature?
Whispers tickle my ribs or mess my hair,
But I am now a pure and sinless creature.

Pure as rain; sinless as money: bones.
Dropped into compost fard and face and flesh.
You don't enjoy me, I enjoy myself,
Attend the various music of my breast
And buss this curious raven, beak to beak.

Pick Up

The sun, a hot brass eye on a ruffian hill,
Blinks at the boatmen. Awnings palpitate;

Stares rhyme. Upon her deliquescent plate
The spoon dilates the lover-coloured ice.

A transformation: tiger-haunted men
Startle gazelles who, pausing, petrify.

Later, when lights dissolve café and pier,
The sun asleep, the speaking canvas gone,

Girls cry to be made flesh; on each white bed
The stone is broken, and the fawn is fed.

A stone her yawn. Sun, over nodding hill
On both our faces, blinds before the kill.

Love Poem

Anvil rang roses, but, much farther off,
Pistons assaulted scenery; the saw
Cut a girl in half, until her mouth bled kisses:
Turbid the chrism of calm in the place of thunder.

Sighs rose like bubbles; all five ancient planets,
Sudden as fireflies, threw, magniloquent,
A handful of gold parabolas – their windfall
Firmament iron the only apples of iron.

Of rosy anvil as delectable star,
A land of never fenced, and nothing sold,
Where waters leap from rocks in smoke and fire,
Each soft riposte an exploration told.

JACK BEECHING

Girl in a Bath

One street-lamp blonde
Put the tongue of a match
To her bessemer hair,

Another mad dish,
Neapolitan jest,
Went out as roast mermaid.

Drop in your bath
Loops of soft weed,
Plaits of sad words.

Mermaids get roasted,
Blondes go in smoke,
My girl turns to water.

Fox with a Halo

Her reasons hid a ludicrous unreason,
Her promises were full of contradiction,
The smile this morning was a lupine snarl;
Our goodbye kiss drew blood.

One handbag full of dollar-shaped dead leaves:
Beneath all that high fashion went bare bone.
This last night was a bucketful of cinders,
The morning froze.

Only huge, naked extravagance survives
The winter blizzard; only sudden death
Puts reason, promise and deliberate choice
In proper attitudes.

At least, a girl; or, last night, was that breast,
Heavy in hand, her breast? Or that hand mine?
Similars kiss with arbitrary mouth.
Whose teeth draw blood, though?

Fox with a halo; sex; venomous broth;
Yet, like the sun, propinquity transposes
Dead leaf, bare bone, a bucketful of cinders
To that handful of warm roses.

On the Death of a Hedgehog

A pot with pampas grass; two assegais;
Under its dome of glass, the Taj Mahal
(One turret fractured). On her corner case
The big Times Atlas; in an upstairs room
A featureless lay figure, for a ghost.

Sun-stencilled pattern of those javelins
Lasted till now; the model tomb has gone;
Yesterday's auctioned house is coming down.
They cut the sash cords, fell the chimney pots;
Peg out the croquet lawn in building plots.

These forty years, how many generations
Had beetle-champing hedgehog, whose last heir
A truck has flattened? Tottered like a lord
Under that red brick wall, would eat the crusts
From sandwiches, but scorned our cucumber.

Nobody, now, is poor enough to wear
Her cast-off clothes, enough the wanderer
To read a moribund atlas. These new neighbours
Grin through each other's windows. Going fast
Her naked rafters. And shall their roofs last?

The Chemistry of Photographs

Passions become the substance of the earth,
Her wanton body a metaphor, even climactic
Mingled cries a child's or migrant's cry,
Or whispering centre of the spiral storm.

Not that, involved in such metaphor, I less love
Your actual body or extravagant voice,
Your fleck of phosphorus, calcium, iron, air,
Quicksilver – once – or quicklime of your kiss;

Nor that this photograph alters – faces turned
In magnesium surprise: the crippled trope
(Mere shadow now her lips and nitrate hair)
Of our private handfast, midnight satisfaction.

Her voice, those voices, soft in the spinal street,
Where a haunted lover walks the long white line,
Loitering out an echo of his lapse
In the bony labyrinth where memory trembles,

Say, these analogies of our bodily vows
Are alibis. Nor flesh nor ghost escape
Prognosis, and the protean sequela
Of kiss and lust: that cry, and yes, this flower.

Love Poem

Catchphrase and downright lie became the noise
The macaw utters when you shroud his cage.
That was the afternoon we lost our tongues;

And lost our wits that day, to live like foxgloves
Belling the air; or cabbages, enfolding
Leaf after leaf discreetly round their hearts.

With razor tickled, with a feather split.
Screwed in a ball the barbed-wire fencing mask,
Missed by a hair's breadth skinning each other alive;

Wickeder than breadcrumbs, breathless, witless,
Dumb as entire darkness, blind as silence,
Lost as two rooftop mice in a flooded river.

Playing the Bones

Man in a spin, or diver out of breath,
Know the sidereal clock keeps different time
From body's invocation and response.

Though vein and tick of time make counterpoint,
Their beat, their pulse, never quite coincide.
Life is what cannot metronome consent.

Where withered aircraft, spinning like a leaf,
Drilled its own whirlpool, lobsterpot of ribs
Lifts in the tide at lunar interval.

Then deaf and dumb your fingers, rosary
The morse of women's bones. That tambourine
Inside your breakfast skull is permanent.

Scavengers

To the impartial beetle, primitive worm
Who keep this world from stinking to high heaven,
The poisoned hawk and smitten fly are one.

Love, when the poisoned hawk, the poisoned heart
Turn, cleansed, and take your hands, what diluent
Rinses the bane? Or, say, what benison?

Because time never turns, venom accrues,
The flux intensifies, the motion stuns.
These hands that touch belong to skeletons.

Talking of Love

Thursday, at noon, the dustbin burst into flames;
A galvanized mistress, hungry after Lent;
Gehenna's bethel; bidet brimming with flowers.
Talking of love, what happened to our love?

(Dead as the dodo or passenger pigeon).
Talking of death, what happens when your eyes,
Helix like candles round a Christmas fir,
Speak poems in a coffin dense with hair?

Talking of us, what happens to our shadows
In this blank noon, or crucifying night?
Will others fall as eaglets out of the sun,
Or trip our feet tomorrow, like dodos or martyrs?

A Dry Little Girl

Give me this day a dry little girl
For a boutonnière.
She may grow in my bath
Like a Japanese flower.

A pokerdice girl
Wrapped in silver paper,
A bouillon cube girl,
All flavour.

Invisibly sweet
As a dab of Chanel,
A stroboscope girl,
An elegant equation.

A girl who is mushroom buttons,
A spoonful of meringue,
A girl who is Greek on the page,
A girl like a deckchair.

I fed a gazelle,
Large eyes behind bars.
She grew into a clothes horse.

Four Limbs One Beast

Four limbs one beast: her black, besotted eyes
In sockets that have no more use for sight,
Collide at last with mine. Whose buttocks those,
Drudging like savage in the ceiling glass?
Rigid and stark her Hippocratic smile,
And now the death, the little death, of love.

So, from this ceremonial mimicry,
Sterile, and wilfully felicitous,
Like priest and penitent we say goodbye;
Having rehearsed, once more, our own last rites;
Brute eyes gone civil, features powdered dry;
Her double doorway like two eyelids closing.

Grey Hairs

Grey hairs are ominous in this wonderland.
Let go the theoretical delight,
Take all that may be captured in one hand.

From mortified money turning, from caress
Dull with deceit, from formal quiddity,
Number the consummations of excess.

All critical gloss and abstract fellowship
Let go, for, in that court, impromptu song
Gains nothing, and is never understood.

Take, rather, doorway clinch, and stairway joke,
Rhapsodic curse, and minion accidental;
The pleasures kiss and come again provoke;

And passion, lifting like a roman candle
All through the animal grapple of the night.
Take all you see, take all that you can handle,

Or intellectual passion, our slow fire:
Her questions rising, like a skein of flame,
His answer, the cremation of desire.

The Child is New

Only the child is new. The kiss on her mouth
Was pigtails in a shrubbery; kiss on her eyes
Unguent, for eyes that wept at their first pleasure;
Kiss at her breast the child, the possible child.

This lore of love is capricious. The virtuoso
Caresses by rote; her devices – wine, candles, music –
Stage properties; the star herself possessed
By her private sensation, her daemon. Can all that be love?

Or is love not the long-abandoned child
Left weeping on the hillside, love perhaps
Head on a breast, the nipple in the mouth,
Oblivion for the day of pain and danger?

Only the weeping child is new, though he would learn
By rote the ritual daemon of your passion,
Lips to a nipple others, too, have kissed,
Crooked in an arm that, also, has borne lovers.

JACK BEECHING

Poem for a Funeral

Who bit the gorilla's ear, having castrated
Eleven rich lovers, littered the city sewers
With her discards, and at random thrust her hand
Into every promising fly, has made her peace.

Her beagle weeps; the hideous parrot, trained
To say come take me, says, come take me; cayman
In the mirrored bathtub weeps a tub of tears.
Her two-legged, fugitive lovers heave a sigh.

Nobody orders candles and champagne.
Priapic statuary, Nippon rubber wit,
Barge poles, tame fish, professional footballers
Take a tumble; her monumental bed is veiled.

Archbishops, excellencies, millionaires
Assemble, envious of her entourage,
The scarred, bald, trembling jockeys, poets, thugs,
The prizefighters and suicides of love.

Amid these stooping men, what desperate throb?
Over the heads of the crowd, what thrilling cry?
She haunts the shrubs at Kew, and Brighton Pier,
Each lonely phonebox, every darkened car.

Three Living

Three living in this room: plant, cat and fire.
Blaze lifts one tawny paw, the prone and still
Cat moves a leaf, her eyelid, to admire.

Kindling consumes, faster than Spring has done,
Such blooms of flame; plant, in your torpid dance,
Take this last light, spat by the lion sun.

The cat explores. Plant has, like smoke, a smell
Not nourishing; the fire spits her way.
Creatures like this are alien, and may kill.

Plant mimes a cat's leap, the solipsist flame
Resembles and consumes, each being fire
In similar forms, and by another name.

Swede on the Beach

And then the kittens come to pirouette,
And then a fat cat sucks the buttertub,
And then the gluebones, and a pair of gloves.

Spatchcocked on ski, two honeymooners leap.
Your alimony whale basks on the shore;
Moths ate the fur upon her pumiced groin.

And then, a clean young man, to rub her back,
And then the fat cat sucks the buttertub,
And shaggy monsters come to join her sport.

Their pussy gloves their other shapes annul,
And then the alum skin, and gluepot skull.

The Mad Old Queer Called Rapunzel

Let down your hair, Rapunzel; nagging voices
Will go away. You've nothing here to hide
Except your sexual pun: derisive choices
Coiled in one carapace; the buried bride.

The man, so far, is dominant; her smell,
For everyday purposes, his. But hybrid gestures
Betray the hermit of the horny shell.
His cloistered woman, hid in virile vestures,

Goes mincing up the stairs; her treble tone,
Gruffly riposted, is their dialogue:
A pariah, chewing on his knucklebone;
The wedlock of a seraph, and a hog.

Look under eyelids. She who dwells inside,
At every blink, is expiating rape,
For this is love: the monster and his bride
Wear the same skin; and neither can escape.

Yet, from this symbiotic doubletalk,
Since any other love is overt treachery
(Ambiguous impulse trips his very walk)
Comes absolute marriage: poetry, not lechery.

Forget the loneliness, the midnight dread,
Those nagging ghosts, that loud and rapine cry.
The one companioned is the comforted:
Your lover sees this desert through your eye.

The Counterfeit Paradise

Assassins, too, may have a counterfeit
Paradise, and why not? The quondam poet
Hugs his false childhood, and the millionaire
His milky tit, a bursting bank account.

Passing within the mountain, they discover
Marvellous women (slaves) and artificial
Rivers of wine; what more can hashish give?
Why blight outsiders with imagination?

Crave, and at last you pay. The murderer
Must push his knife; somnolent millionaire
See hunger blinkering his mother's eye;
The poet be his age, and falsify.

Two Drawings

Near where that obsolete, magnificent
Stallion obsessing Leonardo lifts,
Like mauls, two brazen hooves, an epicene
Ages to slack-mouthed death. His raven quill
Wrote all in absolute line – a kind of love
Come to those pouting and ambiguous lips
Effete as palfreys, and as beautiful.

Waiting on the Bed

Statue a moment in time: the stallions charge.
Wind lifts the hair, immortal hand a spear,
As to that triple mirror, when her eyes
Honeyed the four limbs of a sacrifice
Stretched out like wheelspokes, and her linen field
Altar, or tilting ground; perhaps has stood
Manifold ever since amid the glass,
Shaking her hair, and menacing a hand.

The million sexual analogies
Come to the mind in gesture, and emerge
Obsessively; even the once obscene
Grown normal as indulgent years go by.
Thus piety or power, those doting lusts,
Hermit anxiety, bumboy's phantom pang,
Show former wanton gestures turned to stone,
Fixing their lineaments upon their faces.

And did she come from mirrors to the bed,
Tiger on tiger, spear to welcoming wound,
Dropping her garment like a diffident dream,
Wheel matching wheel, and letting fall her hair?
Horses and riders race along the wall;
The sun marks time, as white clouds pass the sky.
Across this altar, derelicts mime war;
The statues move, the gesturing lovers die.

The Grey-Haired Bridegroom

As their crow-fly rider baulks,
Even pink high-livers fail;
Money talks, but maggots sing
Time the lifers fired this gaol:
All our grossest feeders fast
Since that bluff, unhanselled girl
(Someone has to be your last)
Found her salt-haired lover bringing
Bezoars, the mammal pearl.

Notes for Memoirs

I come to cast my pearl, said Ryan, smiling
Mystification hotter than the news;
Arnold told legends of his ruined arm:
Romantic misery of ambiguous love;
Lies that had some excuse.

Married, or desperate in Istanbul,
Writing publicity handouts, writing verse,
Those brilliant, theoretical young men,
In one sense or another, all are dead;
But there is something worse:

Playing survivor – last one to recall
The joke of drag; exemplar as seducer,
Garlanding statues in a public place;
Lions gone silent; or that virgin torso
Whose shoulders bear no face.

Latent or raving, straight as macaroni
Or corkscrew serpentine, they all are gone
To sojourn in the dark. Each lucid mouth,
Unsated then or since, has sought that girl:
The lie, the verse, the pearl.

Book Review

Of their lives, now shrunk to verse,
Some idiot ambitious don
Writes this scholarly chicane;
On each grave, the facts are stone.
Once I wondered, now I know,
How he lived, so deep in debt,
Where the other got his gun,
Seeking death-by-fire in Spain.
Sick of all this travesty
I assert another truth:
Actions of mortality
Art alone redeems from death.
John and Hugh, brave and true,
Live in what transfigured them:
Verses, fantasies and love.

A Bar in the Sun

Across the bar our gilded dead men shine,
Their blood it was disguised this dust in wine.

Out from the hillside juts a drystone wall
To mark the edge where fields and buildings fall;

There, as the vineyard into woodland turns,
A charcoal burner, burning charcoal, burns.

And so we bleed, fall, burn; so burn, build, drink.
Some think on death, some die before they think.

Four Sections from Long Poem in Progress

1: The Dove

In rings of calm, a dove explores a dome.
Sumptuous once, but now, the tourist eye
Scans a museum on the secular floor:
Ikons three high, and, as the light goes dim,
A torso, where a furtive boy confides
His dolour to her worn and candid breast,
Image of love's dogmatic, limestone sky.

Eyes now turn upward. Guide says, you observe
(Pushing a pourboire in his braided cuff)
Our four unique pendentives – two, three, four.
He warns where not to touch, but does not yet
Ban contemplation: giddy pigeon plays
Theophany; a million coloured stones,
In fierce mosaic, jazz my breakneck eyes.

When all the rest blink impious cameras
Will skied Pantocrator still disavow
A boy who meditates on nakedness?
May he not kneel, to kiss a dove-stained throat,
And, touching that basilica, her breast,
Pray with his genitals – since, like a thorn,
This coloured dome presses on every brow?

Follow the dove, the one free creature here:
The limpid rapture of her indolent play,
Her faith in that umbrella of a sky;
But pigeon falters; doomsday flashlight blinds.
Defeated guide lifts his episcopal hands:
The hot mosaic, a reflective stare
Illuminated, burns me to the bone.

Crisis of self-perception: door is lost
In a palisade of pillars: terror of birth.
Knelt, would they strike me dead? That looming Christ
Must also, once, have known this rift of fear.
His pebble face is blank, yet rosy thorn
Turns as my turning spins the dome, takes root,
Sanguine with bud, in dead and caustic soil.

2: O.T.C.

Death drew a boy's face, when the candle burned
On our gymnasium altar, and all night
His barrack nightmare caught the breath of sleep.
The world can never lose its virtue twice.
Victory gelds; the vulgar lie-machine
Breaks off the grape-vine that was growing green.
Love is the one unpardonable vice.

Distinctions fade, their grey platoon advances.
An apostolical descent of fear,
Holy in stutterer, or sot, or queer,
Might bring a revolution on the street
If guns could petrify a cast of mind.
The city is a bullring in the sun
Where armed policemen shoot the last freelances.

Of two such travesties, the revolution
Might make it new; the new could not be worse.
Though violence, they say, is no solution,
These thumbs and fingers, atrophied with verse,
Flex, as if lifting mortar and grenade.
We, who were told a new world might be made,
One time forsook the cabbage patch, dug trenches.

Yet all have come to this suburban garden,
With flowers like guerrillas, in a planned
Yet truly wild confusion, almost nature.
The Sunday peasant, as the grapevines grow,
Crops the small Eden of his own greensward,
Gives every weed correction from the hoe,
Till his alarm clock lift its flaming sword.

All, gagged in this cat's cradle of abstraction,
Must brood upon an insignificant death
From liberty, deception and conscription,
Or property, taxation, brotherhood.
The soldier dies within the frozen wood,
A jet stream vox humana for his voice,
And, dying, keeps no promise, makes no choice.

3: The Lonely Children

Suppose he held you, under blinding light,
To fill your veins with fire: that man in white
(Your clever son) says, all this pain hurts him
More, in a sense, than you. Appalling glow,
Technical radiance from some place apart,
Concentrates. His hot, malignant barb
Enters the flesh; his silence breaks your heart.

No point to pray. Your white and taciturn heir
Hears cries for mercy as a morbid hiss,
Or evidence, an index of collapse,
Political at last turned animal;
So science like narcotic fog extends,
Mastering means, repudiating ends.
Caesar's real function is to crucify.

The lonely children, having lost their toy,
Hang pussy, and drink madness from the tap.
Innocent, gullible bourgeois, even you
Will die, and when you die, your crazy map
Gives heaven as a city of no joy,
Where conscripts, sent aloft to colonize Mars,
Wait for their limbs to bloat, and learn to cry.

Athwart his woman, someone's fumbling son
Licks the provocative, not yet aware
Language grew up to touch the nub of hope.
His firmament decays in iron sparks;
She caterwauls; and where did rapture go?
Poor puss hangs, full of worms; the maladroit
Bad children come, to wash their hearts with soap.

Their placard's fictive tapestry is torn;
Thirst infinite; identity in tatters.
Now that the sky has fallen, nothing matters
Except this aching in these empty heads.
The seamless garment has been torn to shreds.
The foundling, who drinks pain instead of wine,
Again regrets that he was ever born.

Mad as computers; dressed, like nuns, in white;
Morally-neutral operators crave,
As vivid touches freeze, atrocious power.
Few, of the few who read this, understand:
Not insight or epiphany, mere power:
Are crazy as a surd; impervious
To pain as charcoal tree or nightmare water.

All language turns, though dense and sweet with love,
Incomprehensible. Words full of flame

Occlude my open mouth. What mode of speech
Have torturer and victim but the spasm?
Before this flesh is ash, may one more sun
Bewilder eyes, annihilated name
Shout in wide daylight, and the doves ascend.

4: Words and Deeds

Trapped in the bower of the rubber rose,
Tortured by unprocurable delights,
Noncombatants, their profiles held as trophies,
Watching an enemy at every turn,
Saunter like eunuchs under coloured lights.

Word was a deed, but all the doing's done.
You covenanting lovers, votaries
Of alum rapture or the mirror kiss,
Go, buss a poster face, sob printer's ink;
Not even shadows know what went amiss.

That enemy, become vindictive minion,
Maims, in the solitary, breathless night
With caponizing bomb, and not embraces.
Romantic memory is hermaphrodite,
Haunted by soldiers' as by women's faces.

An obsequy for ghosts, a firework flower,
Since, like black seed, the young and brave are dead,
Their manliness become an artifice:
High mass on that impossible mountain face,
A spinal tremor and a public dread.

Vehement by each livid silhouette,
Candles ascend to mimic hell; his face

Turns pallid on its twin with ardent horror,
Craving the dreaded drop, the final yes,
Convinced his torture measures his success.

Mordant on retina as acid smoke,
Hot dreams of eremite, or prisoner,
Degrade the vigil with a judas kiss.
Only a lover's bodily embrace
Tattoos a never-fading cicatrice.

All human touch, even that meretricious
Cold intercourse in counterfeit of death
Dances with pageantry of affirmation.
Single the passion life diversifies;
Yokefellows waiving love are doubly vicious.

Is that the chilling face his lovers saw,
An English mask, its every lust held tight?
Chin of his youngest child, but for the scar,
Teeth like old sheepbones, eyes the hue of slate.
How has he tugged his shadow self this far?

Crowd to this open, perfume-haunted window
Myriads of Ariels, free as senses die,
Waiting that midnight when the mirror face,
With rigid mouth, comes closer than a flame
To drink the breath, and cancel out the name.

No converse, in that hour, of mouth or limb;
Blind, as a baby crawling through the dark.
The hawthorn leaf turns green, yet has no taste;
The girls pass by, with incandescent hair,
But speech, and this awareness, gone to waste.

Captives of bitter memory, forgive
Your turnkey host: victims of discrete fear;
Noncombatants; philosophers who lied;
Since, by such love, emotion given form,
Annihilation may be nullified.

Gold particles, in spectral saraband,
Throb an erotic motion all day long,
Dust in the sun, this flesh like gossamer.
Add word to word, since words, perhaps, are deeds,
As, knelt in dust, another planted seeds.

HARRY GUEST

A Twilight Man

The black flakes on the quiet wind
    drift through the rib-cage:
Charred reductions of evidence –
    letters, dossiers,
Photographs. The bonfire
    crackles to silence.
Smell of dew supersedes
    the acridity
In back of the heat.
    A wry peace now. Embers
Creep, write enigmatically, twist,
    fade. No messages.
Scraps float, soon lost in the
    thicker air contours abandon.
A skeletal hand disturbs
    the site, prods, stains the
Bone. Faces, afternoons on
    sofas, decisions, success, now
Ash. The head tilts towards the
    stars of slower change
Whose light prickles the empty eye-
    sockets and, dropping into the black
Skull, vanishes, unretained.
    Water beads coldly on
Spine, jaw, poised knuckle,
    and the darkness settles
Substantiate since the last red
    point has gone leaving only
Meaningless wafers for the night to
    obliterate, disperse.

The Summers of Nowhere

Capture the linked hands over a rock
    the shadow eats. Sunfall.
Obsession with camera-angles
    and the diminishing
spill of light behind your blurred profile.

Our forced lips and the night's white blossoms
    echo the lost splash your
bronze arm made – once – water gone, the tide
    swept out and in again,
seasons rubbed on permanent markings.

The dent in the sea, your head's pressure
    under my eye, longing –
the tears on your unchanged expression,
    forever where? An ache
to be naked again in some brown

slanting afternoon. A walk then. Through
    rising avenues of
flowering trees to the ruin in that
    overgrown garden and
the long sea-look over the railings.

My glance near the grain of skin, I brush
    off frequent petals: no
stain – not even light's which greyer days wash
    over. Evening now, our
descent from colour and the need for

warmth shivering over you. My kiss with
    its taste of the moment

ago, the breeze already dying
    which caught every other
word shouted through your laugh from the waves.

About Baudelaire

FOR EIJI YAMAZAKI

I

The dark nerve of sin lay like lightning
on the pavements. Paris was flawed.
The heels of prostitutes tapped open the frost
and a passer-by who existed
and then didn't exist
noticed the world and its reliance upon hell
as circles of gaslight hurried past him.

2

Certainty, colour, in her room. Although
her loins prove as elusive as the sky
and in his arms she twists into a corpse;
all mortality; vapour.

Each time foreknowledge is no help. He knocks,
eager to hold her, keep the void at bay.
The carpet's smooth between the fire and bed.
Time, the old pain, damnation – lost here:
a lift to peace . . . There was
one raging night that squeezed the stars to brightness . . .

The city calls, a fog
drifts around the heart, his reaching hand
discerning worms behind the wall.

3

To rape the air, the dark air of night,
burying an ice-like orgasm in clouds –
thrown backwards on the globe, splayed there,

moist legs apart and her frail perfume
lingering in the nostril. Sunrise.

4

Too late: the schooner's left
buoyant for the golden islands.
His feet echo in the morning;
the docks are empty; a scrap of paper
is blown across the silence and a clock chimes.

5

Sunset immobile lifts the Seine to it:
the past, seen obstinately through the glare,
summons an allegory
and the observer on the fragile bridge between air and air
shivers in the sudden gust
from the wing of imbecility
and the hour-hand of regret starts moving.

6

Now the rain won't stop falling,
the iron hand tightens slowly on the heart.
Now rhetoric's over and the coffin's made
and knowledge of earth replaces mind.

7

But,
in the lunatic's cell,
where whiteness negates the thirst for innocence
and trees stretch their aspiration on pale air,
the fly of consciousness still goes on
drumming against the hard invisibility
until,
beaten by time,

which so insidiously lames the breath,
he gives up and, wondering, drops into
the three-dimensional cobweb that is God.

Villanelle

FOR PETER JAY

Veering towards midday we soon lose speed.
Conviction fails in movements we've rehearsed.
The concentration's lacking, not the need.

The lies we tell can never supersede
A conscious doubt which aggravates our thirst.
Veering towards midday we soon lose speed.

Distracted while experiments proceed,
The charms all crack, the glass containers burst.
The concentration's lacking, not the need.

Somehow it's two o'clock and then we're freed –
The afternoons of failure are the worst.
Veering towards midday we soon lose speed.

The gold sun waits. – When nothing would impede
Our progress to the moment, we're immersed.
The concentration's lacking, not the need.

A new Icarus might yet succeed
Who has a sense of knowing what goes first.
Veering towards midday we soon lose speed.
The concentration's lacking, not the need.

Preterite

TO THE MEMORY OF MY MOTHER AND FATHER

The cat has lost its entity and is,
in the half-rooms of the past, a presence not
a definition. My love for it. A source
of movement. Weight on my absent lap
and fur glimpsed in the dark orchard.

Fewer trees now.

Anecdotes. The gone years offer
abbreviated narrative, the interims
mislaid. Permanently.
                                        From being
partially predictable, the dead achieve
an absolute parenthesis for their actions.

What was a home becomes a house again,
an individual accretion
losing sense at the owner's death.
The coherence goes, as belongings
dwindle into objects.
A drawer full of fossils,
an unfinished embroidery in a sewing-bag,
a diary for 1913.

Toying unnervingly with recollections
we theorize where we had never asked:
ascribe to events and souvenirs
a pattern often meaningless,
the one code that could decipher them
being destroyed.

Key in the water,
the glossary missing.

Names, labels, strut about the past,
obedient as our conversations send them
down grey photographed streets and into
the incomplete gardens.
                              Their substance
being made up only of results,
a conjured memory,
we circumscribe their deeds with laughter,
tenderness, wonder – yet,
before they reach the fact we're aiming for,
there is some gap they don't exist in, a blur
in the foregone outlines.
                              Walking to
the lost hydrangeas, they vanish
ghostlike on the lawn. A hiatus
in the story, unaccounted for, remains
their secret and the way they have attained
a certain triumph of identity.

At Shoreham

FOR LYNN

Nightfall and my hands awake.
A white bird wings upriver,
    Greets the water and
Glides to silence where the
    Scars of sunset heal.

I turn to you, loins bared.
                        Your hair
Floats, blonde on linen.
                        The beat of darkness
Shifts the curtain.
                    Your nakedness
Expects my hands which give you me,
My love, the quiver of my need.

Discovery of your body takes mine out to sea,
Past the safe harbour-bar: last
Reflections of crimson die out,
Diminishing in the glassy walls that rise,
Succeed each other, pass: and the final wave I meet
Brings oblivion, the depth of you.

I lie, cradled, heavy, midsea.
The singing in my ears falls to quiet –
Only the rustle your liquid hand
Makes on my hair.

                Our skins, slowly,
Become familiar. Landfall. We alight,
Moist from the salt, and the one lamp –

Coming nearer to re-create us as a pair –
Dries us to rest.

      The tide recedes.
                 A last wind
Touches the water as your smile lifts.
In my dark breathing you are there. The knowledge of you
Undoes a solitude called sleep.

The river holds the sleeping bird
Nightlong; a section of moon
Flicks at the water, whose profundity
Is tidal, no longer dangerous.
                 Lost time
Passes. The east greys. I stir
To a fresh entity. There is
A swan behind your eyelids when you wake.

The Painter...

The painter,
light dimming,
quits the studio

Leaving noon
to flare at seven,
blossom, vase, sky

Washing the sunlight
from his hands
he enters evening

A caress of colour
inside time
has caught time

Stopped the scissors
closing on the dial.
Separated from midday

by no lie of brightness
the rhetorical flowers
are hammered to the canvas

state themselves.
A match spurts up
and the door closes

Shadows encroach
ink the painting over
while the man

following the tip
of his cigarette
goes down the now dark street

Montage

I swing round the corner, still alone.
There's no-one now at the saluting-base,
and the pavements here in the centre
are all deserted.
                              I wrote once
'Very drunk I raped you and the rain outside
fell on to roses.'
                              The morning lies empty
to another sky, half the street indigo,
half dusty yellow. After so long.

The lamp made your skin glow, at last
naked underneath my kisses. Our year started.

The regime's altered, that I know. A breeze
takes the gulls across the blue gap
between the gutted block of the Royal Hotel
and the bomb-scarred Post Office over which
a new flag strains its colours.

                              In my arms
you were always elsewhere: an absent mouth
soured my embrace. Enigma
of your possession. Once, a tarnished exile
in a borrowed room over a café,
I lay with you on the rumpled bed,
and talked about Axel Heyst, the paperback
tossed on the one table by the cheap wine,
the tooth-mug stained a hard, irregular maroon,
and the cigarette-packets in an alien script.

Months of preparation, briefing, prayers even.

For this. The patient advance by night,
over cold ploughed fields, through the uninterested
villages. Gained confidence. Pre-dawn
in the rain: watches fixed for the attack.
Vengeance on a capital which had for so long
refused to recognize an opposition,
let alone the third party. One green flare;
quick penetration; clubbing
the indifferent sentries; concrete pyramids
across the road; contact with saboteurs;
brief fighting in the squares and the usual
anticlimax. Shirt-sleeved with a bottle
by the shattered fountain. Garlands
assorting oddly with the dirty khaki.
You miles away.

       Some bunting
blows across my path, its rustle and the wind
surround the echo as I tread
the locale of victory, unarmed. There's
the overturned streetcar we used as cover,
the piles of rubble where a ministry was.
Pitted walls here and there still flap
with bygone posters. 'CAUSE FOR ALARM'
'TERRORISTS' '23rd' 'WANTED' 'FORMATION'

When, satisfied, I got off that first time,
pulled up my trousers in the quiet, you'd
already re-arranged the past, contrived
to crown the moment with your privacy.
(So long ago now – noise of the rain – heavy
sense of the summer flowers through
the tang of liquor, perplexed desire, smell
of our rough nakedness and your bruised lips.)

Nowhere to stay, no legal papers yet,
I had to leave you for the tricky streets
at dawn, the danger, no address.
I'd done what I could in service of myself
though you could always champion me
up over roses, violence, still later
the dog's bark in the clogged yard, trickle all night
from the rusty cistern.

                    I can remember
divers codes, the grimy lantern in the farmhouse,
Colonel Hand's eye-patch, the dash for the railway-yards.

You'd skein the triumph out of me and even today
it stirs uneasily at my temples. . . . The odd
moonlight over the curfewed town,
your boredom with my body, our ambitions
altering in subversive pamphlets with their
conflicting rumours of achievement.
And then you yielded to me, all straining gone soft,
your pupils huge, liquid.
                        Reaching the far end of the street
I glance back at the desolation, at
the torn streamers of victory, the empty stands –
frameworks for a memory of cheering.
I move on, turn the other corner.
They are all there as I had expected,
wearing different uniforms, waiting for me,
rifles levelled.

Birth

The first cry of a baby
shakes the stratosphere
making nonsense of
telegrams, reaction

I did not belong
to the ceremony of midwives
pondering here
the desérts of casualness

Wet, blood-covered,
a strange identity
hidden across airlines

Love of
seasons ago
made tangible

Matsushima
(The Pine Islands)

These islands   gathering images
dry slowly from the night
                              Words
comb the pine-trees free of snow
              Saffron limestone
lurching up from the sea-floor,
quivers dripping in the telescope,
              recedes into stillness

Cameras click and conversation
misses me. Before we move on
as tourists (there being
a choice of views from the peninsula)
              our awkward,
isolating minuet
mazes the snow.
                         Death hitherto
was others'
              Metal doors eventually
slamming to on it, the
volubility's boxed up,
driven downhill, leaving
the light to merge into one wet slope
the black footprints
              recalled in prayer
or literature.
              (Now
nothing resembling
smashed windscreens, atomic fire

(Shown the end, 'the
shadow-line traversed': theoretic
security was, the armour,
merciful complacency,
wrenched from me and a shove in the back
had me stumbling in the seismic desert
.... hailstones   .... drifting
gases   .... chasms

)never
reaching the gate to see my wife
smiling in the shadow on the
window of our dark orange-tree
     comfort of books and music
laughter and whisky and bed

     These islands mount the sky

Surrounded by no-one I love,
     a tour a
     microcosm, the horizon
     deceptive,
transfixed as never before
on no future)

          'enisl'd'

               my private mouth goes over
               the dark memory of your body

A semi-colon of death
inside my glance
lends   the islands, my presence,
             that grey salt-beaten temple,
             untrodden snow, shift of conifers
             from colourlessness back to green,
             scud of a gull across the sunlight,
                  all these, the grace,
        a break in them like finality

                        Shops face the water. I buy
                        a wind-bell, some pottery,
                        a necklace

                        wanting that sailor
                        lounging in indigo
                        against the melting quay
                        uninterested stance, bulge
                        in the tight jeans

and not forgetting what I'm not thinking of
        the poems cut in rock,
        theories of Japanese wives,
        the postcards and the ghastly dolls,
        the Zen priests' caves

                        Credible an unborn breeze
                        in mid-Pacific then; green tea,
                        poured, steams near the paperbacks
                        and the vase of carnations; or
                        next year's neon
                        trickling into the cone of shadow
                        between her breasts

We separate
        till lunch
fuses gossip and impressions
    eroded
shape beyond shape
trapped in black plastic,
joining anonymous groups
to be ignored in albums

Fear in my chest, I'm dying quicker now
      memories   illicit
                    sanctioned desires
crowd
      The pamphlet shows
two views from each peninsula
      and disbelief
as an acrid coil of mist
strangles the eyeball
               remains

The islands   along the bay
    horde distance
as growing light assembles
the scooped stone and contorted pine

        Fake, fake correlatives
      islands accrue
      nothing, solving
      sunrise and the flesh gains
      nothing,

73

the fear, Ransome's fear,
stays a lump of pain

the shutting-off of the pulse
my mother knew
    at her Christmas cards

breath halted
my father knew
    'phoning from the darkness

the   gasp, the
squeezed lung, the
heart's irregularity, night
rammed down your throat
I shall know

my wife,
my daughter,

you, you

engulfed, dropped, enearthed

Indifferent, grown hard and ill,
This place we're emptying jostles me

from the tour, what,
emblem, we visited,
my spattered eyes, the gone past,
to, glimpsed, the notes

        fragments, which, slopes
bar of shadow   only half-
remembered   a boat
cancelled by islands
                maybe
                                blurred
tree-trunks from the car-window

desultory, haunted

        are left with, littered,
a complex of terror,
cravings and souvenirs

From My Hotel to Yours Whole Seas Away

Across the bay, from cape to mountain,
winter emerges from the leaves

The cold hotel is silent round my footsteps
Here at the off-season, in a way
under false pretences, having taken
one pace south towards your holiday

The grey sea here shades to your hand,
the warm front curved between us, flecked by darts
Now swirls of vapour thumbprint continents

I imagine you bronzing, my
temporary lover of the ebbing year
My glance goes down the sunlight,
turns after you on dreamed-of streets,
watches you run through breakers, dry on sand

The snowflakes land on spray near the volcano,
whirl round bamboo and palm
The year shifts, opposing climates vie,
eddies of cold drape the peninsula
Shops glow with presents, leather, silk
Crowds at each 'bus-stop, paradox of sleet
on a city built for summer,
and windscreen-wipers cancelling white stars

A rainbow slants over dark hills
The sun twisting through slow clouds
hints at your distance, my
sweet handler of the dying months

You limit me, I ought to try to you
The raw world gleams,
duties conflict as white piles up on green
The old volcano smokes and winter
sizzles into lava

You mould December to our shape,
lathe it to mystery
Clandestine inabilities
committed here and there from openness –
stirred masculinity appraised:
smiles only we can read: taste of your nakedness

Snowfall on frond and the exposed root
Old truths concealed, a recent landscape softened,
hypocrisies made tangible, gold
reminder of your skin shadowed by whiteness

The crater juts, smoke billows futilely
Your held youth allegoried, flame
and toneless foliage

Inevitable frost has no effect

The brightness lifts again. Snow lours.
A bleak marine wind chaps my face.
You'll walk in noon, rose shorts on,
dark glance weighing lust in others; letting no-one
past the opacity before your thoughts

The new year waits twice round the world;
jigsaws of development: snow: kisses,
deciphered only by eternity –
the way your beauty's to be found
in the lost interval between two photographs

The weather yields enigmas to a chart
No rhetoric forgotten, I relate
the past to climate and success to time
And vulcanologists as darkness settles
wait for the earth to speak again

Myths

Behind her
and the other
delicate companions

a yellow sunrise
redolent perhaps of spring

Stepping lightly
on white ankles; blue-robed;
in such slender hands
starred orbs borne

Approaching ever
for innocence, veined breasts
globed with milk

The object-bringers

hawk-
headed, thighed with
plumage, gold
manacles about the arm

greaves stained by red earth

at a half-run,
fleeing, aiming

Light of
sacrifice behind them
Stench of
coiled smoke leaning on a sky

altars reeking

rivulets of blood, feathers,
vertebrae, smashed by the adzes
on to rough stone

The past-bringers

Through the
drifting bonfire's uncertainty,
tall, bronze-loined

Weary with lust, gentle-lipped,
dew on a thunderous cloud beyond them

Praise and
phallic loveliness

The honey-bringers

       illiterate, foul-
mouthed, the hordes shamble, wielding
ripped books, brandishing
sub-machine-guns

     (echoing, the crash of
     celadon, ormolu,
     lacquer frames)

         chanting
the end of history, making for a
final hermitage where one
alone on the peninsula
illuminates last pages

     (short saga in their wake
     of sackings, torture)

Eyes empty of love,
hands hating creation

           The future-bringers

Cold air stretched above the tarn
Under a taut noon
the water quivers

Wind-sung grass laid smooth,
hare-bells shaking

The leering god
wraiths into nothingness, his presence
a faint smear inside the wind

Long, slow approach
from monochromed horizon

No escape now

First
ants; and structure;
discernible; then detail

Those big, daubed, waist-length masks,
assegais poised,
bracelets of human hair, chains
of teeth above the knee

The end-bringers

To Lynn, July

Twice not alone as now
eight months beyond
the hour sperm quit me on
in her unborn the shape
stirs. Her then pierced to my
joy, oval pierced by my
black arrow, cell on cell
webbing history, a
figured crawl from slime
on the way to angels.
Her awareness week by week
spiralling in towards absorption,
the world's alleys gently
one by one sealed off
as the horizon enters
the tips of her hands,
touches her navel, lowered
eyelid. Her presence not
gone from me yet
distracted, sketched gestures
of breakfast, magazine-
reading, attentive ear
to my broadcasts. Gaze
past me, past now, but focused on
the new love in her womb,
circling round me, out from
back to her, brushing my shoulders
with pollen, star-ash, dust
from a butterfly's wing returning:
by-produced gifts to my
blank maleness,
assuring warmth

with casual tolerance,
confirming though
I cannot understand.

Metamorphoses

(Six Poems on Related Themes)

1: Lines for Later

The beauty went half-way. Old metaphors –
now blackmail, hemlock or a scrabbling hand –
no use. Gone, taste of roses, glint
on the eyelid. For wine read lees. As twilight
dividing melody from the usual spasm.
Dream bloodied over, scars
mock hieroglyphics to the pressed
fingertip. Flowers, seemed acrid. Henceforth
bought possibilities only. Musty;
a tarnished mirror in that
echoing house. Apple-cores
round the statue. The garden
of parched lily-ponds in the leaf-browned wind,
given on to. Hidden in scratched
mahogany, private dossier
thumbstained, and photographs
in sepia recession. The held glare
but key to chilly corridors.
Knowing. Watched magnolias
when ephemeral whorls, yes, cream on lip,
masculine twig defying sky,
grim khaki on the gutter. Contempt;
banknotes; third in succession. Crumpled,
dead for spring. A match flaring
again, again, armfuls prepared, what
gladioli even, sections of sun, other-sided
meaning. Cash emptied into the glass
relaying boredom of the stumble up
new and more sterile slopes. Interests crowning

indifferent temples. Contact? Filmed lilt,
the sway into each other's arms,
phrased against by fashionable
dissonance: glimpse through the fog
of bygone tune, the acquainted
formality of shape. Years tolled.
Albums prove nothing me; long pause
attaining moonset and the game of dark.
Through all words, all yearning indicated,
hot mud that might heave similes
to alter daylight. Never. To
retire: black records; shelves in four tongues;
magazines. Goading the clock to synchronize
Schubert Lieder to one afternoon,
paragraphs to horizontal preludes, a comely
lead-singer semi-nude to certain
proscribed concepts: us and love
and liberty. Glance trails the nib.
Hands scorched by the futility,
star shoved beneath the flatness once again.
Short-circuit of explanation,
romanticism at last paid off, stubs
accumulating in the ash-tray,
another spring's farewell to rhetoric.

2: *Photographs of Past and Future*

Love's darkness falls. No allies. I'm. Again
the terrible lucidity. Since God's
condemned to death. Glimpsed, areas concealed.
A newer card-trick brightens up the baize.
Unseen excitements. *White boat summer*. Words
like tropic ivy smother form. Once more
now: armpits, arse-curve, hidden hair. Each page,

longing for revelation, turn, read on,
shows glowing food for peace-time, gossamer
on flesh. And ferns. Lay the long-stalked carnation
near the black wine-glass, enigmatic tile,
green steel. Rest from authority, the gods
vast photostatted creatures on the sky.
No notice. *Flap of glittering wave around
the silence.* Where? A conurbation. Each
responsibility. Ours. Tissued. Gaoled
but by ourselves (*shine of the offshore sail*),
the warder has our face, the -er ending
gaoler/prisoner, the same: outflying fist
strikes our own heart. Anew equivocal
the enemy. Have never dared, hacked through
the thrashing rose-trees, picked the wet toy up,
looked round, gone on. Unended book: the first
coiled sentences enough. The paradox
of ransacking the future for the same
dark daffodils we once destroyed. *Flicker
of sea-light over nakedness.* The laws
torn up but nonetheless obeyed. Their tombstones
grey, noble, flaking, choked, both lamp and angel,
by fancy-coloured leaves. Indicative
abandoned, premonition of the past
forlorn. The chill. (Or blasphemies to scare
the obstinate believer. Realm that each
perception maps.) *A pathless sea; the shoals
not corridors; the signposts, cul-de-sacs;
freedom to stretch the unthronged skies on one's
own peril.* There. And no reply. Felt object
to justify. And something knifes me off
from that, some nothingness. The orchids burnt
by frost. Conservatory forgotten, the
brocade now mildewed in the drawing-room;

the lawn is rank, the fountains smell, upstairs
the radiators permanently off.
Depart for the endless second. Once again
spray fanning slowly, frozen in warmth, the sun
immobilized. A June. The crowds who can't
die either, elbow abstracts, pelting with
busy, unseeing eyes for trains they caught
last week, the year before, a decade hence.
Roar of the surf unheard, weeds of the past
grip with tenacious celluloid, that house,
an uncle, when, what me was that, ahead
a sprint downhill, gash in the cinders, last
questioning glance of terror. *What white dawn,*
marine escape, captured behind what lids
before the emptiness. Extinguished still.

3: Conditional Present

'Rough gale rubbing the trees. Nose chipped,
the statue intermittently
perceived, bay, privet, yew,
copper-green. Once
focus, dead feet for rendezvous,
ground stained, world darker.
Steps dragging. Far. Too few.
If thunder. Wreck the coloured globe
of crocus, dog-rose, creeper,
last insult of chrysanthemum. So;
green. Brown. Estate denuded.
The harder task is grass and mud,
bark, handkerchiefs of sky. To clothe
with night, starless clouds.
The lamp's beam stops
on cornice, grubby mantelpiece,

bare boards, and panes that make
a limit for the light. Eyes closed.
Torch off. Wind sound. Proliferation,
locked up in one's own vividness,
of eddying dreams . . .
Child's hands part the wistaria,
in the fringed gloom femur, skull,
vertebrae; unseeing eyes
locate the tennis-ball.
Retreating laughter. Puzzled
to be here as the game
dies away. Cold silence falling.
Bizarrely, metal, gems,
scattered. Heirlooms lost from light.
Emeralds twisted round grey bones,
a battered crown, dun rubies
along the diseased knuckle . . .
Here in the half-light and not here.
There in the room's consciousness,
storm outside, lightning on rose,
and yet not there. If him,
here, then. Who never was.
Ghosting the self outwards
to printed lives, wreathing
old drawer of papers, younger garden,
clipped blossom shrivelled
in a former room. Whose
profiles, spectral in wrong seasons.
Snuffed. The black, commanded.
Whittling awareness down to here,
this draught, this emptiness.
And conquest partial only: night;
then; ever-present. Re-discovered.'

4: Divers Gods

In the ripped darkness, night's accretion.
Bloom still of self: the baseless nightmare;
visage caught curved on tumbler, a phoenix
circling round no centre.
Obedient camera tracing then
the movement of a thigh. Proud
mouth-slant. Waiting sex
that maddens with heaviness.
Invention. Depeopled street.
Glance clashing, etched smile,
façades, 'bus-stops, alleys,
a proceeded blur. Door-jamb,
pale carpet, curtains rasping.
Obverse, the truth. If eye unmet.
Absorbed impersonally in the throng.
The tensions of worship. Imply
a lone return. Paperweights
posed on a familiar desk
where recognitions still attend.
Imagined fabric forever
unstretched over naked loins. To
attempt again. Wind on the hill,
gorse sparked to sharper yellow, drop
of sheer rain from cromlech to a
disturbed sea. Stamped rituals
on worn moors. In the near-distance
bright cliffs of a retreating glacier.
Stained bones to hack out soil,
weird skins for clothing; ochre,
madder, prefiguring gods
on dry cave-wall, the presences
to come, swirled mist, dark sunlight.

Hard curve through cotton. Slightly moist.
Down on to it, fingers in my hair,
naked past my firmed lips.
Rough this or tenderness? Perform
the same, let him lead. This then,
mouth grab for taste. My hand
works in the sac, hearing
a protest moaned he doesn't mean,
go harder. Am tugged myself,
twisted, wrung. Across
aeons the summoned rainbow.
Whirl down through infra-red
from savagery to savagery,
dance after the ice-age, writhe
on a borrowed bed, the partner exiting
unclasped, never had, illusory.
The storm allows to intermittent silence
in-gathering of selves: memory
or fallacy. The same desires.
Eliminated self surprised
in words, *flash of sea-view from the train,*
advertisements for sunset, evocative
designs of rain. Softer questions
jigsawing more than physical
identities. White splash
on my tongue. What references.
Lumber of spare-rooms, china, astrolabe,
corded encyclopaedias, burst
hinges of labelled suitcases,
crammed escritoire, the aquatints
stacked face against the wall,
wax fruit, warped tennis-racquet.
His sleeping eyelids clamped
on what defenceless I revealed.

Blaze of the sky on furniture,
transfigured dust, random
litter in the unsewn night,
more words, more coloured
photographs, unfinished blossom. The
whirring of tired resuscitated wings.
Thus wakefulness, stirred penis from the scene
of its destruction. Tentative flight
migrates to nowhere. Glass
of garnet wine, brown fingers
on the stem. Skeining the self,
the metal hyacinth remains
diffusing dreams. And inescapable.
Reborn from momentary suicide,
enquiry close to unobserved
experience, constructing
endless futures, endless pasts.
In the ripped darkness, night's accretion.

5: Some Definitions of Heroic

Hemmed in by fire, noting
the appearance of the thing more than
the thing itself. Cut off, the whole
stage roseate, music pounding
as the free arc scorches
nearer, nearer. Heavy gold
ringing my finger, the voice of the god
punishing from the past, committed now
to what is being done. Given
identities based on feeling, hope
leaps from euphoria, humiliations
tempered by irony to a wry
success. Corrective view the product of

sticky day, article read, sudden
laughter irrelevant from behind
made relevant. Oneself that prince,
prat-faller, a pansy Siegfried
past it on a darkening earth.
Belief's ignited: rapacity beheld
as smiling. Tracked. (To where
the long tiger-roses proffer blooms,
maroon and cinnamon, Nile, jet-blue.
With equidistant dreams not quite
unrealized – both, groping in the glare,
have brushed perhaps the semblance of
a similar flower. Aching with sunlight,
loins hard and naked, dazzled,
hair matted, unhearing, encased
in crashing brilliance, and
an inch's separation only
of coursing gold. Impersonal.
Fluent in fire a brighter danger. Leaving
charred aces juxtaposed on forgotten teak –
since trumped by unexpected jacks,
crimson, flaring. And defeat, if that,
prophesied for ever on drab
cyclostyled instructions from
a bureaucratic angel.
(Return to the land of bronze dreams,
mouth glittering with night, my back
beaded with gold dew. More likely,
mordantly, in the blazing garden
a solitary figure shouting
messages to himself; unseeing; 1isible.
The space for unpaid freedom shrinks.
My heart, reviewed, disjoins.
The profile vacillates, transparent,

and, as I gaze, you go. Nurtured,
suicide growing day by day
in the hot-house of the lungs.
Objects themselves take on
positions of command. Geometry:
existing only at
the intersections album
to red midsummer cherry-leaf
makes with the line
from record-sleeve towards
discarded underclothes,
imprint of sex's heat
imagined on the linen. Talk, dead.
Some cool jazz on: in-turned
acidity, the brass and darkness
revolving; development
inside the circle as sound
evokes silence. Whose house
a thought gone always. Again where.
Dared, the doors of mist,
each vision on its own;
oolite and fissure; glimpsed,
the woaded dancer and the rain-god,
boy actor balancing
on slender shoulders what
invisible to him oppresses
adults with the words of tragedy.
And a solution beyond us still
in our control. Fighting down
superiority's arias. The dark
lyricism of hatred. No time
for heroes with their blackjack
of honesty. Discretions. Round
the corner of the yard

sub-tropic leaves provening.
And disallowed. The orchestration
brushed on, soft note on note.
(Following an anonymity
for all the minutes of a street,
tight cleft below canvas belt,
uneven corridor of day
between his legs. The table's
borrowed calm, svelte nouns,
long quiet from trumpet. By-passed
the problems of involvement,
self-respect curdling, their fault,
no guiltlessness, keep the connections clear,
the sudden afternoon, child
and wife asleep, curved on their side,
sun dropping, neighbours' chatter,
trees heavy with summer.
(Hand's-breadth of soft hair between
the jut of collar-bones, in another
thoughtful room, smooth otherwise,
the two coins of flesh dark on his chest.
Legs faunlike, feet uncloven,
languid tool at the end of daylight
a challenge for heroes to unsleep. Guide
to the joy of nowhere, aimlessly;
a honing-down of moments
to extinction. Onus of
step taken, wedlock, issue. Matched
metaphors by themes, the two
irrevocable; ironic
bridges (game and iron thoroughfare)
coaxing duets to yet a re-want;
palmed aces and bribed guards,
the same ingredients of

a different patience with
one flame-singed pack. Shuffle.
New pattern: tramping to and fro. No
exit, despite the use of currency,
past either frontier. Underneath,
the sunset torrent foams. Poised
on no-man's-land. Gossip
of integrity with similar
wanderers. Fugue and shift.
And overlapping time
subsumed. Thickens now
within my grasp. Desired
expense achieving
nothingness. And his. Dissolved.
)Blond)period)wig)doffed,
the silk-lined wolfskin changed.
At last the lights extinguished
to an emptied theatre, no tickets sold.

6: Climbing a Volcano

Justification. Or bygone epics
that support a previous
ignition. Lava-stone
culled over mist, sulphur
dyeing the sun above the crater,
clamps dog-eared notes to a deal
surface. After evening,
grey television-light
and neon couched in plastic throw
illumination on scrawled dreams.
Wind takes the smoke. Perfection,
killed each sunset. Interpret.
Words in no language, perhaps

adulterous thoughts, him gone, explanation
deriving from outdated themes. Getting
merged with other difficulties,
vases and photographs and myths,
such meaningless significance,
the quickened image to belie
a subsequent collapse. Soft rock
and shifting sunsets. Ash all round.
A yellow falsity of light: what was
shored-up romanticism left
menaced. Can who proclaim
without a wound, badge
glory with no relationship
untouched. God's orphans. Stumbling.
The place for wet bracken, noon-coloured
hydrangeas drooping in the green
above, the sundial, gravestone, all
crisscrossed to by questioning feet.
Inside the emptied drawing-room,
phantom of concert, fibres of waltz on waltz,
blare, gloss, as the 'cellos the
tone of exposed chestnut
alter under arc-lights. Weave of past dust.
A burnt twilight. Still
sexuality of filched autumns.
Erotism in black and white.
Boy masturbating. One cool flower,
the purchased vase a coarser blue,
transposed. Private, the sweetness shed
in nervous indulgence, drying
on your cloth, my flesh. Fold
of carnation on itself,
the ceiling darkening, sunset
required. Alone. Extension

nowhere. Rainfall
on non-existent earth, senses
shut off from twenty years ago,
blinded to next year's diary.
Petals now humus. No
welding offered between
the game that might have once been played
and the strange adult streets
you pace on when you've seen
parental corpses lying in the bleak
provincial morgue. Where back to.
What electric thread. None. Memories
disallowed and on to some
ever-created kingdom. Surety
slain, links rusty. Pronounced
guilty of deicide in
the interim between the touch of flower,
the glimpse of nudity, proof of now.
Beneath, always, the piled
mountain. In dark water, shaking emblem.
Areas of love. Interrogated thought. If I
has been destroyed who am.
Débris. All wanted,
vision gone, the orange sun
rules light on every other stair.
Patterns. Cold well-chain pulling up
from nothingness the subsequent. . . .
taste over, slackening. . . . still. . . .
heaved range on the horizon
unassailed. . . . forever. . . . the stone
unrobbed. . . . yet. Frontier closer.

MATTHEW MEAD

Identities

> But the man that is will shadow
> The man that pretends to be.
>
> T. S. ELIOT

> It turned out later that he was
> a fourteen-year-old Mexican
> armed with a water-pistol.
>
> RAYMOND CHANDLER

I

After Paeschendale
After Katyn
After Auschwitz
After Kronstadt
We stand here

After Asquith
After Beria
After Noske
We stand here

What footfall?
What valley what field what forest
What streets in the morning sun
After the streets of Nagasaki?
Mask, persona,
Alias, pseudonym;
We stand here.

Why should we flee Jahveh?
    Where are the lightnings,

The scorched prophets?
'In millions of hearts
'burns the inextinguishable
'flame of his word.'
Apollo: carven flame.
Christ by candlelight.

And that he mount the unbuilt steps
To the unraised altar
   with sky for roof
   and star for pinnacle
   sumus in fide

We stand here.
We stand in the press.
We stand here alone.

2

Will you remember me Tatania
When your map of this country is folded,
When you see no more the low tower and the hills,
The humped bridge, the stream through the osier-holt?

We pause at the kissing-gate,
The spinney twists into evening;
The wind travels far Tatania
And you must follow.
When 'September' and 'remember' rhyme
Shall I rhyme them for a café translation?

The hills wait as always for the caressing eye,
The eager feet of glory or the warning beacon;
Over successive fields, breakers of hedge
Lift to a legacy of skyline:

Will you remember me Tatania
As I cling to these landmarks and scars
Which fade from your mind?

We stand here in the last of day,
The hills wait
The fields are a green sea.
And nearer the light fails
Changes and fades and our eyes
Clutch line of branch
Silhouette of leaf . . .

When Lazarus lies in his long tomb and dead leaves
Tremble in their forgetting dance,
Will you remember me Tatania?
Shall I come like a ghost to trouble joy?
Tatania, Tatania, what will you remember?
Here, with your lips on mine,
Who do you say I am?

3

How narrowly he eyes his sun,
My lamp. And shuffles to the chair
Through trackless wastes of my fine turkey carpet.
Do Bedouin squat and long for shade?
He licks his lips, the mirage left in the cell.

How helplessly his hands clasp
One another; unclip, clench,
Fall palm-down on his knees.
No hand shall reach to bear him up
But mine, fingering the stony dossier.

Paved roads, polished leather, avenues;
Spurred heel, meadowland, the great plain;

Silent they move in the forest; wrapped foot,
Bare foot, claw in the slime;
A wind screams round the naked rock.
He is the rock. The rock will break.

4

We stand here.
Statisti.

My pills are good pills
rustle and chink
container and carton and can
all cars are good cars
but our cars are *sacred*
the next scream you hear will be MAN.

'there is no such THING
        as saturation point'

My pills are good pills
interim interim
dreams you can drive in your sleep
hand washes hand
our after-death service
washes bone-white and bone-deep.

'for Christ's sake, Stan,
        TRY and be a merchant'

Buy it today
that agglutinous yellow
matches the STYLE of your heart
our workers sweat
at contented machine tools
producing the part of a part.

'buy him and THEN he'll buy you'

Mixed in a minute
served in a second
slashes the stomach for days
interim interim
listprice and discount
traders must follow the phrase.

'for all practical purposes
          YOU ARE the product'

My pills are good pills
my self's a good self
complete with a soul to consume
last thing at night
AND BANISH THE IMAGES
don't just say 'Dreadful' say 'Doom'.

We stand here
for all practical purposes
for christ's sake or near offer.
At our heels a question-mark
      in our heads the moon.

5

Am I not also a candidate for fame
    to be heard in song
With blossom in my long
    hair and a sweet name
    to be known by at the whorled ear?
I have heard the roar
    in the sea-shell

and stood mid-water
I have seen one bud swell
    and woken mid-forest
    to keep a green tryst.

Am I not also bound by the boom
    of oaths to love for long
Delay one overlong
    to call me? Whom
    I have seen linger
(it was here)
    by the white wall
    of breaking water
And smile
    as I walked, her truest
    ghost,

And sang and signed my name
    on air. I sing
To be in her song-
    ster-plume
    one feather
Plucked. Am I not another
    candidate to call?
    I walk here
And sing, year-fall, world-fall,
    till the call ring clearest
    in which I trust.

6

Length and breadth of the head
length of the little finger
length of the outstretched arms
from middle to middle finger end;

the porter cannot be sure
the deskclerk does not remember;
and Graebe:
'I well remember the girl
'slim and with black hair,
'who, as she passed me,
'pointed to herself and said:
' "Twenty-three years old" '
and naked, entered the death-pit.
The convolutions of that ear
may not be repeated in history
and if man is the measure of all things
to what assizement shall we come?

Length and breadth of the right ear
length from the elbow
to the end of the middle finger;
each is unique in dimension.
Nevertheless after fifty faces
on the same street, after fifty noses
and a hundred eyes ...
People, Proletariat, Volk –
an anthropometric norm.
Height, length of the trunk
length of the left foot.
The one promise worth making:
    Immortality.

To resume from this dust the loved flesh
as from scorched clay the monsoon rains
wrench a brief tribute of green ...
it is impossible; or that one should walk
from the grave telling of what may be;
or that essence be leached from these ashes ...

An everest of skulls.
An oxford street of tibiae.
If these are the bones of my grandfather
Where is his beard and short temper?
Does he plough the field of heaven
And harvest the golden floor?

Where are the useful, clanking spectres?
Where are the ladies in brocaded gowns
Whose touch was the dawn wind?
He came at dawn in the clean air
In the clear light and our eyes
Fumbled at his face like blind men's fingers.
Length of the outstretched arms
From middle to middle finger end.
Skin-food, 'indelible' kisses, mascara.
Body: metaphor for death.

7

My verses, Ochkasty, and your music,
Your mathematical progression
To the door of Terpsichore's boudoir,
These brought us a summons to dine
At the groaning table of Paren,
To wolf his steak, to guzzle his wine
To play 'feet' with his wife (beneath table)
To ogle his sister.

The hordes of the East are unfed.
I felt them, Ochkasty,
Their hunger a wolf-pack,
Round the broken meats of that board.
Wolf-faces, wolf-bellies,
Landless, arms like sticks.

Most terrible were the eyes of the children,
Heirs to famine; Romulus, Remus unsuckled.

You would share your bread with them and perish,
Remembered by 'Tone Poem: Hunger'.
I am 'aware of the problem'.
See, it clutters a poem.

I weigh our undoubted genius
Against the million-death headline.
I spoon up my onion soup
And know that I am not God.

The hordes of the East are unfed.
If Io herself has failed them
      let us despatch
With teats and feeding bottles
       Paren to lands of morning.

He serves a very good dinner.

He may meet cannibals.

8

I am Morold
already slain

I am a boy
who sings mast high
of another love

I am Melot
the betrayer
to be slain
by Kurvenal

I am Kurvenal

I am Mark
king of a clear grief
and a reasoned mourning.

How then shall I drink
and lie beside you in life
and lie with you in death?

Or are we singing some other opera?

9

Gentlemen of the Geheime Staatspolizei (retired)
and men of other secret police organizations

AND

    that shower of ex-muzhiks
    over there STOP FIDDLING
    with the initials on your epaulettes

        (sings)   you'll always be
               the gay pay oo
               to me

STAND STILL

Now chaps

assuming that his testicles have been crushed,
   his finger nails torn out, his teeth smashed in,
   his nose broken

assuming that he has stood an arms-length from
   the wall for long enough, that he has sat
   on the broken chair for twenty-four hours,
   that he is blind with light, that he must
   urinate every twenty minutes

assuming that the suitable degree of emaciation,
   weakness and subjection has been attained

   that he cannot remember sleep
   that he desires only sleep

SEROV! STOP TALKING ...

Now lads

   if you have seen the ills of our time,
   the disease, its course,
   its deviations

Lads

   is there anything which a good burst
   from a sub-machine-gun wouldn't cure?

10

Marsiglio questions, Hus burns;
Flacius and Melanchthon
       dispute in vain
What the little brown monk really meant;
What is there but loot, von Hutten,
   in riding against the Archbishop?

'Ecrasez l'infame!' Gaols,
Jesuits and salons. Lisbon
   topples: Pombal.
All matters conclude in blood;
What is there but profit, St Just,
 in cutting the head off a king?

And also in Trier, Marx –
Like a Talmudic spectre
   haunting Lenin.
'If you must die what are you dying for?'
What is there but satisfaction, Kinto,
 as the ice-pick splits the skull?

II

'You must meet Julie, oolala'
– and then his hands describe in air
 a form most likely to recur
 with grace this side the last hurrah.

'You must meet Julie, oolala'
– such clicking of the teeth and tongue
 ought properly to lead a young
 Propertius to Cynthia.

Joan sleeps a little earth away,
Lucinda has three sons, a daughter.
Feeling for what was felt before
My hands rehearse their yesterday.

'You must meet Julie'. And I must.
Julie forgive me each faux-pas.
I must meet Julie. Oolala.
So many other girls are dust.

12

The leopard-men
   sang the song
   of the leopard-clan:
   'claw . . . .
   '. . . . . lithe . . . . .
   'soft, soft, our swiftness'
And killed in the leopard-name –
the Great Cat over the Moon.

And that was by night.

So that the day – where they walked as men,
Blunt-fingered, with only a little hair –
Held no ferocity to strike at trivia.
The day was to be lived. Not for the sake
Of night. But for itself. Other than that . . . .
Soft, soft, the shadow moved at heel.

We can fill up the hours with small songs,
Regretting a bright head or a brief beauty
Gone like a night-quenched flame . . .

            'I was seen going down a hill
                    by Edward Arlington Robinson'

There are open streets to maintain by order
Until chaos comes. There is a space
In which to walk as men.
                        To be missed at noon,
The laid table and the expected hour.
Identity is a problem for pretenders.

Star on the night-blue cloth
                    of heaven
Star-son at the pause of labour
    (the birth enrolled for death
    in the pause of piebald day)

Unless he can, wreath piled on wreath,
    Sustain each honour;
Unless he can, plain title and clear proof,
    Speak truly, word and echo;
Each name is grey with breath
                    – an alias forgotten.

13

Not with the gift of frost, fire-delicate on the pane
    – Leaf, stem and flower transcribed:

    'See here the fingers,
    All summer and spring remembered,
    Here set in white, diamond on glass,
    Crystal built in tints of white,
    Here the budding, here the full leaf ...'

Not with that gift; stiffly his fingers trace
Through sham and sweat
    a still-life without reflection;
Or lose touch as memory shifts, corrupt,
Through the half-thaw of noon
    in lukewarm meditation;
Or an opaque pattern
            of transparency
            melts under the hand.

And cold is the element; his fate
To move where nothing stirs
But shiver and apprehension,
To speak with imprecision
            of elusive colour;
He comes cold through many summers
To sign 'Anon'.
                Under a fur hood
Indifferent eyes, clouded breath:
    'Unless the words dance
        you have done nothing'.

Tongue-tip and finger-tip touch silence, zero.

Filigree leaf and star must draw the light
   To their design,
Dead rhythms of darkness
   Dance through halls of flame.
Night must sing in the dawn crystal
   And when the pane is blind with light

All this must be set down.

A Woman of the World

You know the way of the wind
and the breaking bone,
dawn like an early death;

how summer leers – a sheen
composed in a shade.
Shall I tell you

what you know? Does
the dawn-wind bow
and propose
some new truth to the rose?

I bring you a twist of thought,
a pattern-maker's whim;
the iron of your wish.
Queen of illogic
what, except what you know,
is worth the telling?

You know paths over hills
which I have not climbed.
Shall I show you the paths?

You know the curve
of the river.

How shall I lead you
through the great plains
which open behind you?

Echo

1

Except as I speak she is silent. When I speak
She answers in no accent but my own,
Makes her reply true to the last word
Repeating nothing which I have not said.
I speak and she replies. Yet her reply
Lingers upon the word as if the word
Awoke a memory of speech, of how to speak,
Not as I spoke but as she might have spoken.
I speak and she replies. My word is changed.

2

I have said: 'Mere acoustics'. I have said:
'After the word the word resounds
'In accidental halls, chance corridors,
'Briefly incongruous or briefly apt.
'And thunder in the hills
'Is mere reverberation.
'A limp scourge drags the dust,
'A whip cracks empty air'.
I have whispered in galleries contrived for answer.

3

I speak and she replies, making my word her own,
As if I spoke in the darkness of her dream
With the tenuous memory of her speech –
Delaying Saturnia with mischievous chatter,
Calling, disconsolate, down forest paths;
The pool, the broken surface,
The smooth surface unbroken.
I speak and she replies as if we met
With a caress for which there are no fingers.

4

Here let us meet. She has heard this before.
And spoken this, though no tongue
Touch the teeth, though no lips
Shape the sound,
No living breath give voice.

Keeper of many voices, she has heard
All flesh made sigh and stanza.

And now I speak.

There is my word.
There is the interposition of silence.
There is the tremor in a flesh unmade.

Lean Man : Harvest Moon

He, in the swollen yellow light
She lavishes upon the standing corn
And orchards sick with sweetness,
Lifts a lean profile still, in half-reproach,
To her full, bloated face;
And gangling-faithful to his bony past
Sighs for a slender crescent, racing clouds,
In this fat season.

But she, condoning this, most faithful
Through all her constancy of change,
Finding him out of place, predicts a time
When she, a scraped white bone,
Again shall match him.

Only her ripeness will not rot.

Translator to Translated

I. M. JOHANNES BOBROWSKI

River, plain,
tree, the bird
in flight, habitation
and name, strange
to me, never strange
to you – the child's
eye, the soldier's
step, the known
threshold.

I crossed the plain
slowly, saw your fire
in the distance.
Have I set the tree
askew on your sky,
does your bird hover
strangely?
Love
translates
as love.
Her song sung
in a strange land.

An air that kills.

A Poem in Nine Parts

1: A throat constricted in Cherrytree Road

Skirts, head-scarves, skin-tight slacks,
Lips of blood, breasts by e.e. cummings,
Girls hurry up the hill against the wind
To work at the sweet-factory;
It is true that two women
(Furtseva and Pauker?)
Trudge middle-age
Like a theory of increasing misery,
Yet nyloned, sandalled, stiletto-heeled,
Girls hurry up the hill
To hive as worker-queens,
Climbing to an eight a.m. start
With the jounce of a gay proletariat
In a confection of spring sunshine.

This proletariat hurrying up the hill
Is gayer, at a guess, George,
Than any proletariat you have seen.

Hey yeeorgi, Georgi Karpov!
Does the committee still meet Wednesdays
To smash the occasional ikon?

Are all forms gingerbread or icing-sugar
To be munched or melted
Or crumbled into crumbs?

George boy, are things really under control,
Jung untranslated, the patriarch lap-dog still,
The peasants safe in aseptic agro-towns?

Hey yeeorgi, expert in liturgy,
What form of word endures?
Beware George of the whispered response,
Beware of the metaphysics of
      'any other business'.

Head-scarf, mouse-hair, red-head, flame,
Blonde, ash-blonde, suicide-blonde,
The heads bob up the hill
In a highlight of spring sunshine.
Theorist! be subtle
As the shades of Inecto.
Mummd, tampaxt, lyrild, girls
Girded by playtex and twilfit, girls
Hurry up the hill like living dolls.
Today, the consumer market.
Tomorrow, the world.

Lady, your absence is proper,
This hill, I know, is not Helicon.
Forgive me, if having seen men, I pray:
    'Teach women how to prevail'
And then wince at the women.
I have watched with the eyes of a dead man
Who has praised the living
Which were yet alive
And come upon cardboard silhouettes
In the eight a.m. of nothing.

2: A bearing taken on Beechwood Rise

Under the ice-cliffs in the winter noon
following round-cape, glacier edge and inlet,
delineating islet, cliff and talus,

coming on sea-ice clear of jutting glacier,
facing a sudden north, a frozen sea . . .

Plodding across an Anglo-Saxon hell,
the frosty fog like lamp-black on the lung,
an east wind probing for the lumbar nerve,
knowing no ghost by name, no soul by sight,
despising most the accent of the damned . . .

Sitting in draughts, catching the common cold,
crouching upon a claustrophobic hearth,
coughing again, spreading the common cold,
sniffing thick-headed up a chilly stair
to harrow icy bedrooms . . .

Lady, I was content in the cold,
It was enough
To feel the first flakes
Melt in my face
And to lie alone in the long cold;
The frost sufficed and truly
I have forgotten such songs
As gentle the air with your name
And might alter your cold eyes.
I would be silent now,
Walk to my long home,
Sign 'Anon' and sleep
But across gardens, pavements, graves,
A punctilious season moves
Lighting the blossomed tree
And your daughters climb a hill
To become puppets of time and motion
And spoil for a works engineer.

The earth smiles like a girl, assured of her attraction,
Impatient feet stamp the worn stone.
Even I, in cold blood, come to the meeting place.

3: A confusion at Epiphany

Where is the winter queen?
This maiden (no maiden)
Couches on straw. Animal pungencies
Sidle upon the air about creation.

The animal creates the animal,
Corrupts the myth and disconcerts the star.
Where is the winter queen?

These eyes grow large and soft
Not scorning now the stable
And the floor of beaten earth.

Night loses mystery, we see no star.
Where is the brow of snow, the gaze of ice
Holding us in the season which we know?
Where is the winter queen, without compassion?

4: Aide-memoir for an archetype of the Dark Mechanic

carpark officeblock and drive
timeclock yard and railway siding
puddle duckboard rusty castings
gantry on a greasy sky
chimney spout of smoke machine shop
finished plant repair shop plate shop
hammers ring too loud for words.

angle channel sheet and bar
bender guillotine and rolls
forge and burner welder's arc
grinder's comet-tail of spark
foreman office timeclerk jobcard
steward bonus time allowed
hammers ring too loud for words.

jig and tool design and template
cut machine and countersink
centre-lathe and pile of turnings
skim-milk stream of cutting oil
sudden in a greasy silence
teabreak centreforward bonus
rate for job and one off batch.

rust and scale and waiting card
shotblast grit red oxide primer
chargehand holes are out of line
steward strike dispute redundant
productivity convenor
slump and scar and compensation
officeskirt and ringing hammers.

russia management mismanage
walk on concrete work in metal
concrete and metallic world
flesh of wife and fear for children
russia crèche and revolution
rights class job redundant hunger
hammers ring too loud for words.

5: Several ways of ignoring the end of a revolution

Trumpet again the triumph of Soviet steel
Bring back the springing flesh of ballerinas
That the spectre of communism be seen
        only in the public rooms.

*

There is no action but the blind rebellion,
The fingers, closing on a throat,
Seen suddenly as hairy, not our own;
And then our own. And ours the rage
Masking amazement at the broken face
Swaying before us as we strike again.

There is no meaning but the tropic blood,
There is no order but the breaking wave,
No truth but deafness to danger –
The command unheard before the guns speak.

*

Objectively he is a White Guard
Riding across Red Square
To convert the tomb of Lenin
Into a comfort station.

*

When in this monolithic state
I find your dress above your knees
Chloris my rising shall equate
Your needs to your abilities.

*

The doctors are plotting
An adolescent disorder.

*

I have stood in a shouldered square with an elbow
                    raking my ribs
While the metaphor of a slow and heavy beast
                    brooded above the crowd;
I have smelt a shuttered room
Under an open sky.
I have seen the traitor bow
(lick-spittle and alone)
And heard my traitor self
Cheer a proposal to delete compassion.

The great beast, groomed and passive,
Is tethered among ephemeral junk.
My life is a shrunken space,
A furtive shrug before the stupid guards
And clever judges of my acquiescence.

'We have become beggars
'We have been oppressed
'We are breathless ...'
These words will sigh again
Across a stinking square;
And the metaphor charge waist-high.

*

The moon withers in state.

6: A draft for the shop-steward

The ice-men sit where the snow-maiden sat;
They do not understand the cold.

We do not ask for gentler blizzards,
More level drifts of snow, nor that winds
Shall cut us less keenly. We are not negotiating
For mornings without misery nor for afternoons
Lighter at four o'clock.
Thaws at midnight are no part of our demand,
Our argument contains no tropical images.
We want the rate for a condition of cold.

The ice-men sit where the snow-maiden sat,
They talk of furnaces, heating values, insulation;
They would wrap us all in electric blankets.

Into the long cold issues

       a failure to agree.

7: *A dream and a doctrine*

In her first sleep
She stood alone in a high place
Under a crescent of cold light
She stood alone as in a place prepared;
Below a bare summit
Black branches lifted
In withered acclamation.

In the dark dress of night
A girl in a high place
Looked down upon a valley
Churned and torn and silvered
Nomansland;
And knew the landscape as earth,
Earth given to moonscape,

Earth after man, a female desolation,
Earth before star and snake.

She felt herself fade,
Her flesh seek out her phantom;
Sleep was a fluttering curtain
                                torn aside
And night worn threadbare.

Because she does not come
    the girls go up the hill
    keeping the short state
    of blossom-festivals;
Eternity is her measure
  the sun her seamstress.

Because she does nothing
    the girls go up the hill
    against the wind
    into clock-numbered captivity;
She is mistress of the winds
    which serve in freedom.

Because she is silent
    the girls go up the hill
    their sweet flesh, dumb for years,
    crying an hour in exultation;
Her truth is this cry
    shaped to a clear speech.

Therefore, as is well known,
    the girls go up the hill
    and the wind presses on them
    a form of archaic rumour

In which, at her behest,
    the words make sense and song.

Whisper it in the boudoirs of Vitimsk,
Tell it — the hair-driers whine —
In the beauty salons of Shumaisa;
Word for the laundrettes of Harlesden
For the powder rooms of Konitsa
Or wherever, across garden fences,
Runs, barbed, the oral tradition;
Hear O ye cities
And discussion circles at Chofa:

    'Because she does nothing
        she is nothing'.

She dreams.
She has dreamt you.
It is enough.

8: To a poet a thousand years hence

Mine is a voice for quiet rooms,
I think that you may not hear it;
A managerial Apollo does not hear it
And it is unadvised by me
That Mercury recommends dividends
Which do not comfort Pluto.
Councils of state, ceremonies of death and birth,
Strike meetings, learned assemblies
— at all these am I silent,
    absent and silent, not a slurred
    vowel, not a bitten consonant.
Mine is a voice for quiet rooms

Where, to the manner born,
A girl may ignore the drone of my small heart.

And you have bathed and come with full belly
To warmth and suave light
And to this English text?
Lenin and Stenka Razin
Simbursk bleibt Simbursk
The night breathless
          with nightingales
The orchards white with blossom ...
Or a circle of hungry dark
Squats in the woodfire's flicker?
The machine tool has damaged the psyche;
Stalin, O sunken sun ...
Honours fall thick upon me
   as wreaths on the brow of Bukharin.
We meet, if we meet, my friend
In a wilderness of yellow pages.
A thousand years is as long as death.

Mine is a voice for quiet rooms.
I sit in rooms thick with music
I counterfeit silence
And set this word on the evening wind:
She is the snowfield, the blossom,
The song you sing. Like a deliberate archaism
I think that I bring you no news.

9: A six o'clock shadow

The first dusk drifts
through the lights of the shopping centre
veiling the girls who wait,

their reflections poised in plate-glass,
for the heavy date.

The first dusk drifts
by appointment to counsel love
that enchantments are what they seem.
The one tree in the street is heavy
with ornamental blossom.

rockabye baby
the world goes by
to nightfall and neontime
rockabye baby
the world goes by
wait in the doorway
and see if he comes
and if he knows why
the first dusk drifts
and his banner over you
is ornamental blossom.

The first dusk drifts;
gaze in a darkening glass,
you are not made fair in vain;
you are made fair that blood
rise to the call of trumpets
beat with the wild drum
that singing break forth
at agate windows
that pleasant borders
be rich with song
that midnight lie weightless
sharing breath and meaning.

The moon renews her light.
The song made new on lips
that never sang before
(as in Verona, here)
sings of the first and highest
Mother of mothers,
fathered without fault;
here as in Delos
her sure sign crowns the night
as the moon renews her light.

We sing beneath no green tree
and beside no speaking stream
but amid the steel, glass,
concrete of conurbation,
yet though we play by ear
we have the song by heart;
hear us, mistress,
hear us in this city
and hear us
whether these black stones
   stand or fall;
we sing at one with all
   which cries to be born.

Lady, 'young-as-ever', thrice-potent
to cause, to measure, to fulfil,
for this night are we false to our day
   and 'our age' cracks.
Mistress of fortune
   preserve our fortune,
Ruler of darkness
   prepare a death

for the flesh which sings now
makes moan and shivers silver
as the moon renews her light.

The Young

Here they come singing
        into the wind:
  'When the wind rests
  'We shall rest'.

       *

Ho Fiona, lady of three summers,
We have sung wordless songs together

(a unison of sheltered places)

We were both older than they.

       *

And one need not hear to know.

The woods sweep down to the edge
Of history. The axe is blunt
        in my hand.

       *

Northwest all day.
Twice at my back.
Twice in my face.

Whispering in the branches
Of such ancient accord
Such true concurrences
                              No doubt.

                    *

Here they come singing:
    'When the wind rests
    'we shall rest'.

Seeking no calm.

Since the War

He stands up

A wet leaf
    brushes his face
or a dry wind
    defines him

his feet
    in sand
his feet
    in mud

faraway mud
    of which we know
    nothing

He stands up
your beloved son
he moves forward

Little men
    of another colour
        kill him.

A Greeting for Sophie Elizabeth

The cry of birth,
The smell of blood,
Small things;

Good for us,
Bad for General Motors;

Welcome to our concern.

MATTHEW MEAD

In the Absence of the Muse

And you have waited a year, a whole year!
They sit there, the others,
Bones bleached, black sockets staring.

And you have waited a year, a whole year!
In ten cities they were deceived
By a conjured apparition.

Sit straight, write truly
Or stare into the night,
Each footstep may be hers,
Each hand on the latch hers.

From a Provisional Capital

1

Hang-dog, amnesia-like, the air
Sags like a long-unanswered prayer,
Sprawls solidly across the town
To send blood-pressures shooting down,
And clamps an ennui, undefined,
On the blurred edge of hill and mind,
Collapsing, a besetting sin,
To seal a river valley in.

All such a climate can require
Of men is that they quickly tire
And live on sleepily, content
About a seat of government
Where a grand coalition sours
Within its temporary towers.
Here staring blankly at a page
I met my early middle age
Thinking a thought I'd thought again.
This is no country for young men.
Here memoirs mushroom in a mist
Where might-have-beens may half-exist
And automatic stanzas run
Their course beneath a clouded sun.
A perfect frame for apathy
Stretches as far as one can see:
The aftermath of blood and soil,
No KPD, no Jews in Beuel.

2

The female circle shifts, changes,
Five women, four women, six women,

I have sat there, one man alone,
Three women, two women, four women,
None of them quite past bearing,
The same faces and the changing faces,
One man alone and the bodies dust
Beyond Orel and Tarhuna.

Apartments too new
For ghosts to guess their way;
The rooms identical but differing.
I have sat there and smiled, I have seen
The circle of thickening waists.
I have missed the men
With a touch of grey at the temples
And thirty years to die.

Two women, four women, three women,
Missing the flesh gone for ever,
Alone in the sagging flesh;
I have sat, I have smiled, I have seen
The gaps in the shifting circle.
Sleep on beyond Lemberg and beyond Vinnitsa!
Shall I write your dialogue for you?
'I'm bored.
'Where are the children?
'We're going home!'.

3

Cities rebuilt; like scars.
The goddess has no name.
Who but she rules, three-fold,
The thrice-divided land?
I am the barren man.

A third of alien speech,
A third of dogma, dull
With double-talk and death.
And what do they mean here?
I am the barren man.

Who but she, wholly one
And treble in intent,
Rules the divided land?
I am the barren man.
The goddess has no name.

4

A life continued like late afternoon
After an early afternoon of love.
Why wake, why rise to sleep-walk in the sun,
Why cast the languors off?

The armies are bonemeal on the great plain,
The blood is washed from the Atlantic shallows.
What terror will be stricter than our terror?
Destruction more destructive? Who will strike?
What defence stands that was not once cast down?

Sun in my eyes, strong sunlight on the pillow.
A life continued into separation.
What further ardour can the day demand?
Wait for the dusk and hunger,
Long shadows, slanting light.
A face and breast in profile against sunset.

5

When my words have been true
                    for ten centuries,

When age after age is consoled:
        'Well in that ruin
  'one at least found fortune,
  'his page embraces her still'
And in Kurdish or beyond Kumara
My words call you back from death;
And you come; and I never tire of calling ...

Face to face, the night made flesh,
facing the dark in their place,
sprawled, lulled, sucking sweet air,
we lie in place of the dead,
named, known and knowing,
a darkness countenanced,
dawn never to come

When they seek the place
through the dark, faceless,
only knowing light has failed

When they lie in our place
their flesh made night
dawn never to come

Know then, as now,
I shall not forget.

Ten centuries true to the letter.

Love. The cold day.

6

In Rhöndorf bleach distinguished bones,
At Dollendorf the vineyards cease;

A pond, a castle and two swans,
Bad Godesberg will keep the peace;
The river passes, flowing on,
Leaves Königswinter to the Dutch,
Skirts round a government and Bonn.
Schwarzrheindorf has a double church.
The century and season slow.
'mouth to source pure'. *Spätlese*. Tense
A great negation builds its No
From decencies of decadence.
No more. No longer. That was then.
The dark mechanics wreck the state.
The hills and villages regain
Importance for a later date.
Late, less to say; a sinking sun
Throws shadows down to meet the dusk;
Crow, charcoal, death; the colours run.
Late, less to do; I watch the mask
Of twilight fitted to the day.
A woman veiled - the eyes unseen,
The lips unkissed - who moves away.
And green is now the darkest green.
Late, less to need and less to give,
I listen where I spoke. I wait
To hear the last diminutive
That light may yet enunciate.
A wing unfolds, a line of black
Joins earth to sky upon the height.
A nameless watcher turns his back.
And silence takes the shape of night.